D0873307

WILDWOOD,
A Forest for the Future

by Ruth Loomis

with

Merv Wilkinson

photographs by Neil Aitken

REFLECTIONS
Gabriola, B.C.

ISBN 0-9692570-6-6

Copyright ©1990, 1995 by Ruth Loomis
Second Edition

Published by
REFLECTIONS
P.O. Box 178
Gabriola, B.C. V0R 1X0
Tel. 1 - 604 - 247-8685
Fax 1 - 604 - 247-8116

Printed in Canada

Table of Contents

Quotations following chapters are taken from public input statements made on PROPOSED POLICY AND PROCEDURES FOR THE REPLACEMENT OF MAJOR VOLUME-BASED TENURES WITH TREE FARM LICENCES chaired by The Honorable Dave Parker, Minister of Forests, at Island Hall, Parksville, B.C. on March 10, 1989.

Introduction

I drove down Yellowpoint Road, on the way to Wildwood Tree
Farm, with the car windows tightly closed. A rotten egg smell permeated
the air, drifting with the prevailing winds from Harmac pulp mill four
miles away. Large areas of clear-cut logging, done recently on private
land, made the smell more pervasive. I turned onto a side road which
exited into Wildwood property. Large second growth trees quietly
welcomed anyone driving towards the house.

When I arrived at the gate, it was shut. Merv Wilkinson, the owner
of Wildwood, must not be home. He usually left it open when expecting
me. I got out of the car to swing open the gate and sniffed—not pulp
mill, but skunk cabbage growing and blooming in profusion in the low
areas of his property. The smell was pungent and alive.

I continued down the winding road through Merv's forest, huge
trees lining my way. The moss under them was thick, covering rocks and
fallen branches like a green snowfall. I parked in front of his hand-built
stone and log house nestled a few hundred feet from the edge of
Quennell Lake. An orchard of fruit and nut trees separated the house
from the chicken coop. Sheep grazed in a fenced-off area and three little
black lambs rushed back to their mothers as I opened the car door. Merv
wasn't home but the porch light burned. He probably wouldn't be back
until after dark. I switched off the car motor. The frogs, croaking
blissfully in chorus, persuaded me to take a walk during that peaceful,
transitional time between sunset and darkness; the long twilight of a
spring evening.

Here was fresh air and peacefulness, an oasis. The large trees of
Wildwood Tree Farm exuded life-giving oxygen, and the moss-lined
roadways quieted my steps. The animals trusted the man who shared it
with them, for they too had found refuge. Merv told me many accounts
of deer, beaver, eagles, and hawks. This spring a cougar stalked the
sheep at lambing time, leaving paw-print signs in the damp earth.

One evening he told me of his new discovery about the pileated
woodpecker. "Do you know," he laughed, "Those birds keep ant farms!

If there's a nest of ants in a dying or decayed tree, the woodpecker will 'harvest' them. He won't clean out the whole nest, but leave enough so they'll regenerate for a meal later on. But, on a healthy tree, those birds will go after every ant . . . won't leave a single one."

As my walk took me near the lakeshore, ducks scooted off and six Canada geese came honking in for a landing. Even the decaying stumps, part of the surrounding forest, were beautiful in a covering of fungi and lichen. They had never suffered the charring forces of a fire which inhibits for many years their decay and eventual return to the forest floor.

Wildwood also has its open fields abundant in wild flowers and meadow grasses. The place is as it should be, I thought. It is for humans, animals and plants together. The harmony gave me much to ponder as I walked a trunk road back to my car. The evening had faded into a tranquil darkness, but the quarter moon shone between the spires of the grandparent trees that had reseeded this land for hundreds of years. To realize that the 136 acres called "Wildwood" had been logged eight times since 1945 and has earned its owner a third of his income makes most other methods of forestry shameful, if not criminal.

I sat in the car contemplating some of the facts and figures Merv had given me: The original cruise of the stand when purchased in 1938 was 1,500,000 board feet. The volume cruised in 1985 was 1,173,250 board feet. The cut since 1945 has been 1,378,292 board feet. The stand will REPLACE its original volume in another two and a half years. The plain truth of the matter is that with care and understanding, a forest is harmonious and productive. The sad fact is governments continue not only to allow, but encourage the policy of slash and run tree "harvesting".

That evening Merv was elsewhere on his property preparing for a ninth cut. With his abundant vitality, his days are full. Whenever possible he takes the time to go ocean "cruising" in his canoe. He is an avid paddler, interested in west coast native cultures, and in rediscovering the nature of their beliefs. "Perhaps there is a reason I am a paddler as well as a forester," he mused as we browsed through the book *My Heart Soars* by Chief Dan George. "The native people knew they were not separate from the trees, but part of everything living on this earth. Canoe-making was a spiritual involvement. The tree carried its spirit to the sea in the gracefully carved canoes which travelled the coast."

Now Merv is taking advantage of the long daylight hours to get his work done. Soon he would be off to the west coast with canoe and tent, another reason for being his own boss, a citizen forester.

Merv has had hundreds of people tour his property. Many naturalists, environmentalists, foresters from other countries, school children and journalists have learned about his carefully managed tree farm. All this takes time. He is happy and at ease sharing what he knows and is learning. He was interested in a book about the philosophy of Wildwood, one which would endorse and encourage alternative forestry methods. In recording his words and taking many more walks through Wildwood, I learned that Merv's instinct and compassion for this forest was right because I too felt happy and at ease among the trees.

For anyone fortunate enough to own a wooded parcel of land, *Wildwood, A Forest for the Future* encourages you to maintain, utilize, and live with your forest. That means, as Merv says, ". . . working with nature. Then you have a constantly growing 'garden'. It gives you an income, and a home for yourself and the wildlife. It is a place of peacefulness and harmony."

Ruth Loomis
April 1989

"And I submit these three principles, basically: the first one is give thanks for the environment . . . summarized by the word 'care'; the second one is, use the environment wisely, and that's called 'stewardship'; and the third principle is trade or barter any excess and that's what we call 'economics'."

—K. Sturmanis, Kwakiutl District Council

Pileated woodpecker ant farm.

A Little History

My 136 acre tree farm, "Wildwood" at Yellowpoint near Ladysmith on Vancouver Island, is a sustained-yield, selectively logged tract of timber that has been producing forest products since 1945, and will continue to do so indefinitely. Here, there is still a forest and it is growing faster than I log it. I make a good living without destroying the forest. I work with nature. I harvest trees periodically for specialized products and on a regular basis for lumber, enjoying the forest, and its tranquility where all the living organisms are present and healthy.

I grew up on the edge of an undisturbed, natural forest. At the age of seven I was playing a game of peek-a-boo with a half-grown cougar kitten around a big log in our back yard. My mother decided to break it up with a broomstick. She was a dead shot and could have stopped the game permanently, but the kitten was quite playful and really quite harmless. The animals, the birds, the variety of trees that grew in that forest beyond my yard were a source of wonder to me then, and have remained so ever since. The forest was very near and very dear.

I grew up believing that forests are my friends. They are there to use. They are there to enjoy. They can be maintained. They should never, never be destroyed. If we are to have any forests left in British Columbia in fifteen or twenty years, it is absolutely necessary that we change our methods of logging. It is equally necessary that we change the thinking of company and government Forest Service bureaucrats. I do not want to be around when the last forest is gone. Rows of trees are not forests. They represent blind stupidity and a one track mind.

History teaches us about the errors of man, and I was very much affected by the analysis of historian Edward Gibbon in his book *The Decline and Fall of the Roman Empire*. He describes what happens when a nation neglects its natural resources and impoverishes its soil. The Romans, nearly two thousand years ago, logged Lebanon, North Africa and the now barren Aegean Islands by the same methods used today. Clear-cutting was just as devastating then as now, and most of that area turned into a desert. The Athenians, by the 7th century B.C., clear-cutting to supply the building of warships, lost their forests.

Libya is only now beginning to get a forest back, improving its climate and its agriculture at the same time. Like the Greeks and Romans, we in British Columbia are creating desert areas. I decided long ago that I would not work towards such destruction.

My own operation started almost by accident. In 1936 I was fortunate enough to buy a parcel of land with old growth trees of mixed species on it. Times were tough. I would not work for the forest industry so I had to face the problem of making a living off the place on my own. I went to the University of British Columbia which had some short courses in poultry and livestock. I thought I might learn something in agriculture for survival. While at the University I met a professor of agriculture from Denmark, Dr. Paul A. Boving, who was a trained forester in Scandanavian methods. He found out about my land and suggested I crate up all those ideas about poultry and beef and "do" forestry. He had taught forestry in Denmark and Sweden before coming to Canada, and since there was no faculty of forestry in Canada in 1938, he became my private tutor. He put me through a forestry course that gave all the basics in practical forestry and assisted later in my completing both practical and theoretical forestry. Upon completion of the exam, Dr. Boving gave me my graduation paper. "Don't think this has made a forester of you," he said. "It has only taught you how to become a forester. Don't stop learning now!"

I have learned many things since then, many things he would have liked to have known. I became an expert faller, a logging operator, and a forester—all three necessary to maintain Wildwood Tree Farm. Unfortunately my methods and those of the professor from Denmark are not those taught today in the universities or in the industry.

* * * *

"I know with all my mind and body and feel in my heart and my spirit the land I came from; I know my relatedness to it. I am bruised and wounded by the clear-cutting of the forest and the destruction of the habitat of all the creatures who live there . . . ."

—Renee Jackson, Citizen

... forests are my friends.

January, 1995

In the five years since the first printing of this book, Wildwood has become a learning experience as well as a working forest. Now I find myself a teacher as well as a logger and a forester. People are coming from South America, Europe, and the United States to get knowledge from me and give knowledge to me. Above all, I see that universities may or may not be good in their forestry instruction, but classes can never replace experience in a natural forest where common sense and intelligent perception prevail. As was pointed out by a forestry professor at the University of British Columbia, 4% corporate funding has affected 85% of the curriculum. This does nothing for good forestry.

It's Sustainable

Wildwood Tree Farm is a place where sustainable, selective logging is practiced. I must emphasize SUSTAINABLE. Selective is not good enough. I've met loggers who claim to do selective logging. This usually means that the best trees will be selected for cutting and the rest left with little consideration for regrowth or future production, certainly not for aesthetics.

Sustainable means "to sustain" or, to keep the trees in production, sustaining the level of growth of the stand and never over-cutting that growth. These 136 acres grow between 500-700 board feet per acre per year which gives a potential harvest of 68,000 board feet of timber each year. During the 1985-89 period, Wildwood grew 270,000 board feet of timber. When completing my ninth cut in January 1990, I had removed the 270,000 board feet. I count anything over six inches in the growth factor, therefore I must include any wood used for fence posts, firewood, and shakes, along with the milled timber. This is sustainable forestry management. Really, in effect, sustainable IS selective. A forest which is utilized economically cannot be sustained without being selective. The two are interdependent.

Harvesting of the trees can be done in cycles or continuously as long as the proper percentage is taken. I never cut over the annual growth rate, as that breaks into the "bank account" of the tree farm. It may sound like business financing, but consider the forest the "bank account", the annual growth the "interest". The "interest" is converted into the products which are removed from the forest, but the "account" is left standing. I have now learned to leave 5% of my "interest", or annual growth, to decay and rot on the forest floor, a reinvestment in the soil, a reinvestment for the future.

Unfortunately, in British Columbia, the big companies have been allowed to over-cut, abandoning any idea of sustaining. The Department of Forestry claims that in 1988 the forests grew 74 million board feet during the year. The cut during that year was 90 million. I have heard that the more correct figure is 108 million. Is there any worse "deficit financing" than that?

The tree farm is a garden. The produce comes out of a garden every year. My "produce" comes out every five years. The only difference between the garden and the tree farm is time; time which allows the growth to become marketable without the destruction of the forest.

In order to keep the woodlot sustainable, it is necessary to understand certain fundamentals to have healthy, happy, and productive trees. These fundamentals I follow on Wildwood Tree Farm. I know the annual growth of the trees. I understand species-value according to the land and terrain. I thin for light and growth to encourage the proper canopy. I let reseeding occur naturally. I must take care of the soil, making sure enough woody debris is returned; and I consider carefully the factors of road building and erosion. I provide myself with a good income in terms of time and investment.

The basic tools needed to operate a tree farm, or woodlot, are minimal compared to other businesses. The common denominator for good sustainable logging is to work WITH nature, using good, common sense. I have a double-bladed axe, one side for chopping at ground level (which may dull the blade), the other, which is always sharp for use on the trees. I have a power saw that is comfortable to handle and I know the fundamentals of using one. It is not a toy, but a wonderful tool that must be handled with care.

Walking through Wildwood I have learned to observe the growth and well-being of the trees by the length and color of the leaves, and the condition of the bark. In forestry, the learning never stops.

*   *   *   *

"Woodlot owners of the land are becoming leaders in applied environmental protection. You cannot have a sustained yield without a sustained forest."

—Harold Macy, President,
North Vancouver Woodlot Association;
Secretary, B.C. Federation of Woodlot Associations

The tree farm is a garden ... my produce comes out every five years.

January, 1995

I have completed the ninth cut at Wildwood. The total volume removed from my forest is 1,672,000 b.f. as of October 15th, 1994. I have started the 10th cut and an additional 70,000 b.f. has been taken. A detailed tree count and partial analysis done during August, 1994, indicates the original volume of 1,500,000 will be present at completion of 10 cuts. Experienced German, Dutch and American foresters who have studied conditions at Wildwood, point to improved soil and better spacing as the reasons for a 10% increase in forest productivity during my 50 years.

I now realize the original amount of debris left behind after cutting was too low. Listening to fellow foresters such as Chris Maser, Herb Hammond, Orville Camp, and Tim Foss, I am now leaving much more especially large faulty pieces which show decay and are really not suitable for a product. These become nurse logs, home to bacteria that aid the soil and new seedlings, critters which live in the hollows, and fungi - that very important element of our forest biology. I cannot extend a rule book about debris, but close observation as to the soil humus gives the clues.

Soil: The Real Resource

A forest depends on the quality of its soil. The soil consists of many things: the organic matter and plant nutrients; the sub-soils underneath which provide the trees with anchorage and mineral intake; the bacteria and micro-organisms; the fungi and the bugs and critters that aerate the soil. It is a balanced entity, so that if you destroy that balance, you're going to be in trouble. In assessing Wildwood's soil, I analyzed it for three major factors: texture, drainage, and organic material.

There is little likelihood of improving soil by a short process. Chemical fertilizer is only a stimulant at best. It is like a shot in the arm to a drug addict. The effect of chemical fertilizers is very minimal and can have the disastrous result of stimulating a tree, then retarding it. If fertilizing is continued, the soil will be damaged and the result will be poor quality timber. Fertilizer might be used only in very special situations where there is temporary stress on the trees. It will keep them on "hold" during a disruptive project. Even in that case, the value of chemical fertilizer is questionable because the soil can become further damaged by the killing off of micro-organisms.

The size of particles beneath the composting, organic layer gives texture to the soil. The largest particle size is sand, which is gritty; next in size is silt, and then clay. Most species of trees are tolerant of a wide range of soil types. Here are some general observations:

Douglas fir, pines and cottonwood are most suited to sandy or gravelly soils.

True firs, (amabilis, grand, sub-alpine) and cedars love soils with sand and silt.

Spruce is happy with a base of silt and clay mixed.

Hemlock wants a well-drained soil with a top layer of organic matter.

Humus is a necessary ingredient of good quality soil, just as it is in a garden. I never discourage "unwanted" species on the land. In fact, contrary to many forester's way of thinking, I don't consider much as unwanted species. Alder, maple or willow add humus, through the annual shedding of leaves. By protecting soil from evaporation, more moisture is saved than the trees use. The willow produces a great deal of compost with the dropping of its leaves. It doesn't suppress the growth of the young evergreens. Its foliage is not dense, nor does it grow very tall.

"Soiling" plants are plants which add nitrogen to the soil, particularly alder and broom. Broom grows on very poor soil converting the nitrogen (which is "fixed" with the help of bacterial action) so that other plants can absorb it, leaving a much improved soil.

One notices that bush alder comes back first on many slide areas, holding the soil so that trees have a place to grow. Alder can make a good cover crop, and as a tree it has commercial value. If allowed to become too dense, it can retard the growth of seedlings. Alder, however, dies off quickly. Thinned and spaced, it can provide an ideal protective cover and speed up the growing of the seedlings. The question here is, under that type of management, is the soil ready to bring the conifers to maturity? With the help of a friend on Saltspring Island who is using alder in a rotation to conifers, I am studying this question.

Leaving biodegradable waste on the forest floor is the most effective way for improving soil. The best biodegradable waste is that which comes from the trees themselves thereby ensuring that nothing is introduced which will upset the ecosystem. Branches, leaves, needles and log sections should be left to rot. After a cut, I care for the soil by allowing forest litter (branches, unusable parts of the trunk, rotten wood) to go back to the forest floor. Organic material on the surface indicates how quickly decomposition is happening. However, if there is more than 10 cm. of organic materials (often true in swampy sites) tree growth will be slow.

The burning of slash is the worst crime perpetuated against the forest soil. The average soil building rate in North America is one eighth of an inch every hundred years. If a man-set fire is burned over this, it destroys the accumulation of many centuries of topsoil. It is the topsoil that grows the trees. The subsoil provides the anchorage. If the topsoil is destroyed by fire or scarifying with heavy equipment, causing erosive water run-off, the potential for growing a new forest is lost. Retrogression then takes place and only the primitive forms of plant life grow, such as mosses and lichens. The damage of man-set fires is very great.

A natural fire, such as one started by lightning, usually happens in a forest that has not been cut. The soil in that forest retains much more moisture than the soil in an area which has been stripped. A wild fire, in a mature forest, is never as devastating to the soils as a fire set in a logging slash. The wild fire will not kill all the main trees. It does kill a lot of the undergrowth, but often only the part above ground. While the bush looks ugly, frequently the root systems are not dead. The fire forms the basis for a terrific downfall of organic substances. With the help of bacterial action still alive in the soil, fallen needles, singed leaves and bushes will rot. This is a platform, a compost, for new seedlings. Because there is the added impetus of potash, phosphorous and nitrogen, and there is still growth to hold the soil, the new seedlings often appear within a year and thrive.

People travelling this province have seen the terrible examples of erosion due to careless, thoughtless logging practices. Clear-cutting, burning, stripping, and exploitive road-building all contribute to the loss of topsoil by erosion. In order to get the water to percolate instead of running (which carries the topsoil with it), a good forester will have trees and underbrush left, even after he has logged. This is what selective sustainable logging is all about.

Plant and tree roots hold the soil in place by draining it of water. Roots (tubular conductors of water), insects and small animals create pores in the soil which hold air and water. Our current logging practices reduce or remove most of the natural biology of the forest and uses heavy equipment which compacts the soil. Excessive run-off and erosion are the consequences. The roots of plant growth in poorly drained soils, become water-logged, shallow and stunted. Dry, fast draining soils leach out nutrients quickly, also affecting the tree growth.

In working Wildwood's forest, I planned the roads to protect the soil. Road planning is as important to the woodlot as a foundation is to a house. If the roads are well constructed and not over-used, damage is minimal and accessability a real asset.

Roads are necessary to extract forest products, but if built incorrectly, the drainage and erosion caused by fast-tracking water completely alters the nature of the forest area. For example cedar, which desires a considerable amount of moisture, could find its roots too dry because of altered drainage; Douglas fir, in the way of a large amount of run-off, could "drown". The combination of clearcutting and road building contribute enormously to the erosion of soil.

My first task in planning the road network was to do so on paper, following these guidelines:

(1) Make use of old road grades

(2) Follow contour lines wherever possible

(3) Identify sites for decking (log storage for truck loading)

(4) Keep curves on minimum grades

(5) Avoid areas that may catch and hold water

(6) Avoid unstable soil conditions.

Selective sustainable forestry results in a tremendous saving in road costs. Due to repeated use of the same roads, the amortization goes down with every cut. By the end of my ninth cut, the 1.25 miles of main lead has cost 29 cents per foot. Future cuts will further reduce this cost.

Since it is unnecessary to bring in large equipment to Wildwood, the dimensions of my roads can be minimal: a 10-12 foot wide main road with good shoulders; an avoidance of sharp curves (each curve needs a 4 or 5 foot clearance back from the road so the end of the logs can swing) and no grades over 10 degrees. Skidder trails, which connect to the main road, are only 6 to 7 feet wide. If I ever found an area unsuitable for skidder machinery, I would use horses. They need only a width of 4 or 5 feet, can pull out anything that a small skidder can manage yet are very manoeuverable. There is now a tremendous interest in horse logging which avoids the destruction of heavy machinery.

I have tried to keep my roads to a minimum. I even vary the skidder trails, sometimes letting the ones used in the last cut grow over if the erosion is evident. One can see that selective, sustainable management allows for such variables. A new skidder trail made for another cut is fine if I can utilize the wood that is removed.

In one place on my main road I had to cross a swampy area. I used a method known as "punching". I pushed down into the swamp some junk cedar and ran equipment over it to pack it down, then put dirt on top. I have two feet of cedar slabs under the dirt and the road will last for many years as long as the wood stays wet. Punching is very economical. Roads going across muskeg were built this way. Another name for it is "corduroy road".

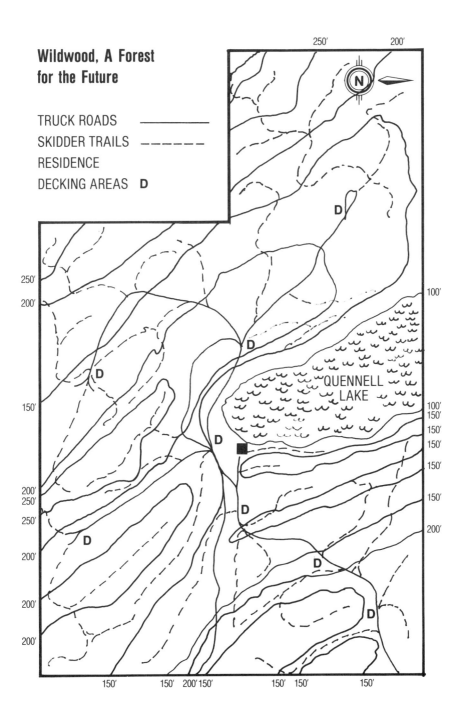

Wildwood, A Forest for the Future

TRUCK ROADS —————
SKIDDER TRAILS — — — — —
RESIDENCE
DECKING AREAS **D**

QUENNELL LAKE

Good roads are built in the spring. By fall everything is settled and
packed. A good road grade is not over 10 degrees and slants toward the
bank, avoiding valleys or draws by passing the end or mouth of them.
Every road made destroys the productivity of that part of the forest, so of
course, the less road making the better. A canopy overhead diffuses the
rain and protects the surface of the roads. Driving into Wildwood, one
feels the protection of the forest which thrives on its natural soil
conditions.

* * * *

*"Our forests are suffering from overcutting, poor road
building and inadequate reforestation. Our forest management
methods drastically reduce fish spawning areas, wildlife habitat,
tourism, employment and what precious little old growth forest that
there is left. We are heading for a colossal disaster . . . ."*

—Ray Hill, Citizen

Branches, leaves, needles and log sections should be left to rot.

In the summer of 1994 while teaching in Oregon, I had the pleasure of meeting Dennis Martinez, a scientist from the Navajo people. He is also a shaman, having studied plants and the use of fire with his elders. Mr. Martinez is doing phenomenal work in rebuilding forest, scrub and range land in the South West United States. He has a very valid case for the use of fire in some forms of regeneration. Anthropologists refer to this as "landscape burning".

In British Columbia, the Indians were the first game managers, discovering that openings in the forest cover very often resulted not only in a better crop of berries, but also a larger population of deer. Huckleberries, raspberries and Indian potatoes all benefitted from fire. In the early 1880s travellers on southern Vancouver Island reported burning done by the Salish people. Miles of ground was burnt for regeneration of berries and the camus roots. Some of the small islands in the Strait of Georgia were individually owned by Salish people who, after digging the root, burned the ground each year. However, the fire in all cases travelled quickly and was of low intensity. The Gary oak and the hazelnut also benefitted.

Dennis Martinez carefully pointed out that giving this tool to "White Brother" was not wise because "the aboriginal people used the accumulation of knowledge vested in the Elders and the Shaman who have a very good knowledge of weather signs for the area to be burned ... my White Brother would be too likely to use a wrist watch, the calendar and a rule book." Oh, for much more wisdom and less regimental stupidity!

The Seedling

The natural growth of Wildwood is managed, yet reseeding is left to nature. The planning of parent seed-trees has been a fascinating process. Why have I chosen certain trees for regenerating the land? How did I know it would work? Why not cut the lofty parent trees for their wood products and replant with commercially prepared seedlings? Here I am back to my number one rule: Work with nature! Invariably "nature knows best", and my instinct says nature's ways are vastly superior to human ways. Since I do not clear-cut, there is no need for mass replanting. I have staggered my parent trees through-out Wildwood in prime positioning for regeneration. I am managing a forest, not a plantation.

The cones of the evergreens start to dry in the fall and scatter with the equinox winds. Cedar and balsam cones don't open until they have a good frost—then the seeds fly with a little weather vane. After an early snowfall, such prizes may be seen lying on the surface of the snow, food for the hungry birds and chipmunks. A tree 150 feet tall experiencing a 5 to 10 mile per hour wind will seed an area a thousand feet in diameter. A moderate wind of 15 to 20 mph will extend this to a half a mile, and a strong wind will double that!

Some of my best trees are parent trees. They are the ones that show strong growth, free of genetic defects with good quality cone production. A tree needs to be observed over several seasons before it is selected, to see that the cones are abundant, well-developed and not misshapen. Undeveloped cones signal that an aging tree has lost vigor. I have chosen the best possible type of each species, located in suitable soil conditions: fir on the drier locations and cedar where it's wet and moist.

Trees start naturally by finding their own habitat, doing it very well through a process of elimination. Wind, rainfall and weather help to regulate the growth. There are early signs if the growth of the seedling is not vigorous. Then I step in and manage by eliminating the real "strugglers" or deformed trees.

Natural seeding always takes place under a canopy. The "canopy" is the overhead branches and crowns of the growing trees through which light is filtered. Trees 40 to 50 years old (approximately 75 feet in height) make excellent canopy. To be successful in natural growing, there has to be the correct amount of light. To avoid becoming bushy, the trees need to reach for the light. This encourages long, straight trunks, with healthy crowns and minimum size limbs. A safe rule is half light, or half the light a tree would have standing by itself in the open. This varies according to species.

A good forester manipulates the canopy, opening up and letting light in when necessary. A suppressed tree, one not growing vigorously because of insufficient light, will release (gain a good growing pattern) when sufficient light is returned. There is no reason to remove a "light suppressed" tree, and lose the advantage of its early growth period just before the volume gain. Let the tree "release" by thinning neighboring crowns or selecting the mature trees near it for removal in the rotating cut.

A canopy also protects the seedlings, diffusing heavy snowfalls and hard, early frosts. I know the normal rate of growth for this area and know, by simple observation, whether a tree is suppressed (not enough light) or forced (too much light). Enough light to make the tree grow; enough shade to make it reach for the light, is the rule. This is key to the success in Wildwood's regeneration.

In the case of clear-cutting, where there is no canopy at all, seedlings that survive look like Christmas trees. They are bushy and as they get older, crown off too soon. These trees are shorter, with heavy butts, short taper and lots of knots. This kind of growth is for pulp wood, not timber.

A tree that has been transplanted needs eight to ten years to be completely clear of shock. I have seen plantations where the seedlings seem to have survived the first shock of transplanting, but eight years later the small trees go into another shock which eventually kills them. This is not due to salal or insects, but often because of intolerable light and soil conditions.

To show how trees grown under a protective canopy reach for the light, I did an experiment. I grew seedlings on a strip that had been clear-cut and other seedlings under canopy adjacent to the clear-cut. The seedlings that were protected showed 15 percent more growth, at the same age, over those in the clear-cut. It makes one wonder, doesn't it, about our future "forests", plantations, fraught with problems. The idea that regeneration cannot happen under canopy is a total myth perpetuated by those who want all mature trees cut for economic gains. Has nature been wrong for thousands of years by regenerating under the protection of parent trees?

In fact, nature is so determined in her regeneration that trees grow out of stumps and can be manipulated to do so. This is called "coppicing". A tree stump is kept alive by leaving its root system intact in order to produce more trees. A tree is cut high enough to leave intact one or two good limbs, preferably on the north side of the stump. These limbs will turn up reaching for light and fill out into another tree. Some people produce an amazing number of trees off one stump. I've seen eight or ten trees produced off the same stump. It is a way of keeping a healthy root producing for many years. If the parent tree is cut at a fairly young age, there is a good growth of branches nearer the ground and each of these branches are trained into trees. The process may be repeated when the tree that had been formed from the original branch is cut, leaving another branch which in turn grows into a tree . . . and so on. The root system is growing bigger and bigger and enough coppicing is done to take up that energy. I have produced some very high quality Christmas trees coppicing in selected areas.

The best coniferous species for coppicing are balsam, fir and spruce. Hemlock does not seem to respond well and pine is questionable as it reacts quickly to any cut or wound. Coppicing is also very appropriate with deciduous trees. Maple, arbutus, and birch will sprout from the root (another form of coppicing) if the parent tree is felled when the sap is down. I keep the best sprout or two to form the new trees, a marvelous way of utilizing a well-established root. I have an arbutus that I have coppiced three times, each cut is used for choice firewood. Alder is the one deciduous tree that does not respond well to coppicing, but reseeds itself naturally.

The diversity of the forest safeguards the future of Wildwood. I see the conifers and deciduous growth above ground contributing to the cycle that happens below ground. Nature equips these trees with the genetic ability to adapt and survive. I am not interested in planting genetically manipulated stock which jeopardizes the resiliency of Wildwood's forest.

* * * *

". . . after clear-cutting, how do you replenish that forest floor . . . the animals move out of there because there are no more trees, the mushrooms and fungi aren't there anymore because there's nothing but often burnt out stumps . . . I'd like to know how that is replenished so that you can reforest?"

—Joyce Stewart, Citizen

... Natural seeding always takes place under a canopy.

The Forest for the Tree

There is much to learn about the basics of a forest, especially with new information from biologists and scientists showing the forest as a whole ecosystem, not just trees. Because I love the forest, I have tried to maintain Wildwood as a whole unit.

A forest is underground as much as above ground. Scientists such as Chris Maser and Dr. J.F. Franklin are showing us that what goes on below ground is basic to the well-being of trees. When I started Wildwood, little was written or known about the forest soil as far as foresters were concerned. Incomplete knowledge led to wrong assumptions and poor practices, the worst being clear-cutting and burning.

The forest includes the soil, with all its interdependent bugs, fungi, burrowing mammals, ground-covers and undergrowth, the trees themselves, the birds and animals living in, or moving through it, the natural water systems and the air. The basic cornerstones of forestry are soil, water, air and sunlight. One cannot be separated from the other. The death of one part is the demise of the other. And let there be no mistake about this—there is no such thing as a decadent forest! The old trees here, my "grandparent" trees, have a function. Even after they cease to grow, their decaying process is essential to the life that is supported on the snag as it stands, and to the life and soil it feeds when it falls. A forest is not just the trees anymore than a house is the roof. I have one Douglas fir that is at least 1800 years old. It still spreads seed. It still releases oxygen. It is still growing. The dictionary says that a forest is a large growth of trees and underbrush. It is much more than that. It is a process of interrelatedness. Knowing that, I am very aware of cause and effect and the relationships which are constantly changing. I am reminded that not one thing can exist in a forest by itself. As I walk through and manage Wildwood Tree Farm, that fact is uppermost in my mind.

When I started the study of forestry in the '30's, much was known about a "tree" but little about a "forest". A tree grows upward and outward as it matures, with new growth added each year to the tips of the branches and the top of the crown. Each year, a new layer of wood is added, becoming a new ring. The roots form the anchorage, and bring soil nutrients into the tree. The trunk acts as a pipeline between the roots and the crown. The crown manufactures the food to fuel growth. Of course, there was more of a breakdown in my studies covering the manufacturing of the tree's food through photosynthesis, the use of carbon dioxide and the release of oxygen. The root system subdivides into finer and finer roots, ending with single-celled root hairs which act like sponges in absorbing nutrients.

Now some of the most important new discoveries regarding the interrelatedness of our forest life are being published and reported. For example, there is a symbiotic relationship between certain fungi and plant roots. The fungus will form a mantle which covers the root tips. This fungus is an extension of the root system, absorbing nutrients, nitrogen and water from the soil and transferring them to the plant. The fungus produces growth regulators and enhances the tree's resistance to attack by disease by producing compounds that prevent disease contact with the roots. Chris Maser describes the role of fungal mycelia eloquently in his book *Forest Primeval:**

> *"As the mycelia grow into and around the root tips, they also grow out into the soil, where they join billions of miles of gossamer threads from other fungi. These mycelial threads act as extensions of the seedling's root system as they wend their way through the soil, absorbing water, phosphorous, and nitrogen and sending them into the seedling's roots. As the seedling grows, it produces sugars that feed the fungus, which in turn is nourished by and nourishes the seedling. The tree is a product of both the sun's light and the earth's darkness; the nutrients of darkness feed the top of the tree in light, and the sugars of light feed the roots of the tree and the fungus in darkness."*

How do some of the spores of the fungi spread? Maser studied the fecal droppings of deer mice and red-back voles, who dine on mushrooms and truffles, passing the spores intact through their intestines!

The word that is essential to our understanding and studies of the forest is "interrelatedness". Do the corporate boardrooms which manifest profits by clear-cutting our forests understand this? I sometimes think their comprehension of "interrelatedness" is simply the growth of profits "interrelating" with the economic well-being of the stock-holders. Such profits are taken from old growth forests in which the corporations have never invested time or care—old forests that existed before the time of Christ.

* * * *

January, 1995

Plantation forestry first took hold in Germany about 200 years ago. Germany has very deep soil compared to any forest area of Canada - 15 inches to 1 inch of our soil. It appeared that all forestry problems had been solved. You simply planted, grew, and harvested. Three-and-a-half planting rotations later, the forest has been devastated. The Germans are desperately and methodically working at rebuilding them. In the last four years, I have had nearly fifty technical forestry people come to Wildwood; biologists, soil experts, and wildlife people. One biologist stayed here, working 9-10 hours a day, studying the plants and soil system. Her work is now on every forester's desk in Germany.

The German foresters who have visited Wildwood, some with 20-30 years experience, like the continuity in management. Most important, they like the wholeness and integrity of the forest, small as it is. One of the senior men, Klaus Gros, remarked "This is not only a working forest. It is a forest that works!"

Germany is now growing hillsides of red alder, an enormous step forward in rebuilding their soil. Alder supplies much needed nitrogen for the next generation of trees, (Douglas fir in our case) and has a very important role in the biodiversity of the forest. The Germans know it is not a nuisance tree. Unfortunately, many of these superb foresters have written me that contacting the forest service or corporations as to the many ideas generated at Wildwood "is a waste of time, and we do not have time to waste ...."

Forest Primeval by Chris Maser. pp. 19-20. Copyright © 1989 by Chris Maser. Reprinted with permission of Sierra Club Books.

... A forest is underground as much as above ground.

Reading the Rings

A fascinating part of my forestry practice is "reading the rings". As a child, I loved the history stored in every tree we cut. The rings showed age, growth, happiness or stress, for the tree rings act like a crystal ball in reverse. They add to our knowledge of what a tree likes for growth, and even tells of weather conditions decades ago. When children come to visit, reading the rings of a tree tells the natural history during their great-grandparent's time.

The annual growth rings of a tree are those circles within circles inside the tree. In the spring of each year, the tree creates new cells in an area called the "cambium" just inside the bark of the tree. It encases the tree in a sheath from its roots to its branch tips, and has the amazing capacity of growing in two directions at once! Cells of the cambium grow toward the bark (the outside edge) and are the carriers of the tree's sap and sugar. As they are pushed outward by the formation of new cells these "carrier cells" thicken and die, becoming part of the tree's outer bark. The cells produced on the inside edge of the cambium form the waterway of the tree. This is the "sapwood". As the tree grows in diameter, the inner most cells of the sapwood become clogged with resins, oils and gums, losing their moisture content. Now this part of the sapwood changes name and becomes "heartwood". In the very center of the rings is a soft core or "pith". This is the oldest part of the tree.

The outer bark, inner bark, cambium, sapwood, heartwood and pith are all the living support system of the tree, its trunk. This is the "wood". Each growth ring in the trunk represents one year in the tree's life and it is possible to interpret much of the tree's life history by "reading the rings".

In the spring of 1989 I decided to take out a tree that was under stress. Looking up through its branches. I could see too much sky. That meant there had been a thinning and shortening of the needles. There was a mossing over where the needles were not growing properly and more than a usual amount of lichen. By studying the bark, I saw it was not expanding as much as a healthy tree.

After the tree was felled, the rings showed its growing history. The last fifty years I could verify. The total age of the tree was 145 years. During the first third of its life it had very fast growth, but the quality of the soil at this site depleted, and after the first fifty years of its life the growth slowed down. By the time it was almost 100 years old, I bought the land and put a road through, changing the amount of moisture the tree received. Trees close by crowded it, further retarding its growth. When these were removed, the tree was "released" and even with the interference of the road, it again grew rapidly. I changed the road pattern 10 years ago again reducing the moisture to its roots. The rings show stress during the last ten years. Another interesting find in this tree is a double ring in one year. A double ring indicates a warm summer, a very cool fall, then a warming again causing it to resume growth—a double growing season!

The beginning of April until mid September is the growing season for this climatic zone. As the weather turns colder, the tree "hardens off". If it warms between late October into November, the tree will resume its growth. It is no wonder there is concern over future climatic conditions. A warming trend, such as the predicted greenhouse effect, will change the whole nature of our forests.

Outer rings, as they grow, put pressure on the inner circles, making stronger wood. The annual growth ring is made up of two bands of cells, "springwood" and "summerwood". In the early part of the growing season, water is plentiful, growth is rapid and the large cells are created with relatively thin walls. This is the springwood. The later summerwood cells are slower growing, smaller and thicker-walled. The summerwood cells are stronger than the springwood, therefore lumber with the greater proportion of summerwood will be stronger. This tree had a very good proportion of summerwood before it became stressed. If it had continued to grow in a healthy way, the inner circles would have been much more compressed.

Just to see the marvels of our trees, look what happens to the rings of a tree which has been pushed or changed some way from its upright position. The annual growth rings compensate over the next few years to bring the tree back to its original vertical position. In conifer species, the tree develops a type of "compression" wood ring. The wood in the rings are larger on the underside of the tree to effectively "push" itself upright. The deciduous tree does the opposite in the same situation. It produces "tension" wood rings that grow larger on the upper side of the tree to "pull" itself upright.

Reading the rings of any tree tells the history of its environment—its food, water, climate, stress, injuries and ability to adapt. In order to obtain information about the growth rates of my stand, I needed to know the age of the trees. This I did by using an increment borer (a type of auger which when bored into the centre of a tree, takes a small core sample of the growth rings) or by cutting sample trees down. The understanding of Wildwood's growth rate by reading the rings is essential to maintaining a sustainable yield.

* * * *

January, 1995

Reading the rings improperly can lead foresters into a massive trap, one that has been part of our forest policy. In the cut and plant rotations, present policy allows, even encourages, the harvesting of trees starting at sixty years. Most trees show thicker rings during the first 60-100 years. In looking for a quick fix, the forester says, "Cut that tree," because he assumes it has made its best volume growth. Hold it! Between the ages of 60 and 240 years a Douglas fir makes a terrific gain in volume. Remember, each ring must add growth around the tree all the way to the top.

A 240-year-old tree has 26 times the volume of a 60-year-old tree. Vertical growth begins to modify at 150 to 160 years, but volume growth continues. In the 1992 value pricing of $0.20 per board foot, a 60-year-old was worth $7.20 while a 240-year-old brought $187.20

Old healthy trees are by far the best producers of forest volume. I have not been fooled into cutting 60-year-old trees because of rabid ring growth. The volume of large healthy trees is the key to a superb volume cut at Wildwood.

... Looking up through its branches, I could see too much sky (tree on left).

The Volume and the Harvest

The growth rate for Wildwood is between 500-700 board feet of timber per acre per year. Since trees and soil vary in this stand, I had to section the 136 acres according to growing regions and take the average growth rate in order to know what I can remove. I do not want to reduce the basic volume of the standing timber.

In this district, a better than average growth on a tree is a foot per year. This can be achieved in a forest of 250 trees per acre where the density of the stand regulates its growth. A ring sample showing six to eight rings per inch is good timber. This information is necessary for the management of a sustainable woodlot.

Once I know the volume of growth, I have to decide on the periods of cutting—every year? Every five or ten years? Generally I make a cut every five years. Based on my volume of growth, I extract up to 340,000 board feet of timber every five years: 500 b.f. x 136 acres x 5 years = 340,000 b.f. I stay on the conservative side of my volume growth. Anything that I remove from the property over 6 inches, such as fence posts or poles, I count toward the annual growth. If I fill special orders in between the five year cuts they are also deducted. Balancing my cut against the annual volume growth is very important.

How many years will it take the forest to replace its original volume? I know in the 25 years between the ages of 50 to 75 years, a tree will treble or quadruple its volume. The idea of cutting a tree at 50 or 60 years is pretty crazy as each year after that age, the tree really puts on the volume. The "rotation" cycle, or the minimum life span of a growing tree, should be 75 to 150 years old. The original plan was that this mixed forest would replace its volume in a 75 year period. After fifty-one years of management, Wildwood is already close to that goal, needing to add only 326,250 b.f. to bring it up to the original 1938 timber cruise of 1,500,000 b.f. This will be achieved in the next two and a half years. Since 1945 I have extracted 1,378,292 b.f. of timber.

In Wildwood, there are some trees I won't touch, even though they're ancient by forestry standards. However, I do cut "over-age" trees which are still sound but are not putting on volume and retaining only 50% of their needles. They are winding down their life cycle and are not strong enough to be parent trees for reseeding. I also remove diseased trees. These trees I've had under observation, aware that the growth is curtailed. They still have useful wood. Damaged trees with broken tops (which can become hosts to disease) or a tree that has been wounded by a blow-down striking it, are also removed. Genetically inferior trees often having club tops (a mass of limbs formed at the top before the tree has grown normally) or marked bends, are cut. It doesn't take long to recognize inferior trees, and I do remove them from the stand.

Wildwood produces a variety of products: firewood, fenceposts, shakes, Christmas trees, pulpwood (though I have very little), specialty wood, lumber and plywood. Fourteen milling operators have drawn timber from this forest and several of them a number of times. Cutting involves one faller, a yarding crew and a trucker. I do the thinning, pruning and culling myself, along with the falling. I have earned one third of my income from this forest in the 51 years of operation, investing twenty to twenty-two percent of my time. If I had five or six hundred acres, the Wildwood type of management would keep two people fully employed, plus a crew and trucker at falling time. The full value use of wood at the mills would increase the employment of many wood workers in British Columbia.

Contractors are eager to return to my operation, certainly an indication that they like what they work with. Selling the timber has never been a problem. If there is the slightest rumour that I'm about to cut, I receive calls from the mills. The quality of the wood is very competitive with the giant forest companies and even the hi-tech mills have been eager customers. Very few trees go for pulp as most of my trees are valued too highly for that market.

From my own experience and the results I have attained, it is obvious to me that this method of forest stewardship is a clear-cut alternative rather than the clear-cut rip-off we see in our province. If we are to have any forests left in B.C. in fifteen or twenty years, it is absolutely necessary that we change our methods of logging. It is equally necessary that we change the thinking of company and Forest Service bureaucrats at the same time. Blind stupidity and tunnel vision is no longer acceptable. It is a fact that more and higher quality wood has

been taken from this 136 acres than if it had been clear-cut. It is a fact
that Wildwood will soon have again the same volume as when the
logging started in 1936. It is a fact that Wildwood is still a forest.

* * * *

January, 1995

Canada uses the metric measurement in the woods. I stay with board feet
(b.f.) to prevent confusion for the reader. Metric measure perpetuates
deception as to the true state of forestry in B.C. and Canada. When
comparing Ministry of Forest figures for annual allowable cuts and volumes
harvested, a report for one year can be in board feet, another year in metric!
It has caused the building industry a headache, especially since Canada has
not totally "gone metric".

My ninth cut removed 293,708 b.f. The tenth cut is in progress and
preliminary cruising indicates the volume is nearly on target with 1,500,000
b.f. left as growing trees.

From B.C. to Texas many similar systems of sustainable selective forestry
are doing very well. I visited two or three of these operations. In Mendocino
County, California, 14 families are logging and ranching 9,000 acres. They
have added-value products produced on the land - oak flooring, arbutus
paneling, and furniture to name a few. The products are sold in their own
store and everybody is employed. In Alturas, California, 7,000 acres have
been in the same family for three generations. They have practiced selective
sustainable forestry since 1888. This family cuts the oldest trees, something
I don't do, but they have a different situation. The trees in their forest -
ponderosa pine and sequoia - seed heavily between 25 and 30 years, while
Douglas fir and hemlock wait until 60 to 70 years. They have the same
volume of wood as in 1888. The examples go on - 4,000 acres in Lorane,
Oregon, employs two crews full-time; Orville Camp, in Medford, Oregon,
has kept his 288 acres in constant operation for 15 years. Scott Ferguson,
in Oregon, manages 154 properties with four crews. Scott thinks a 40 to
60-acre plot is the most economical as it requires only one road. The
similarity of volume produced and the similarity of systems were both
interesting and gratifying - operations that have been maintaining themselves as forests for many years.

... I extract up to 340,000 b.f. every five years.

The Panic Button

A visiting forester wrote me, commenting that he had noticed disease in some of Wildwood's trees. He advised me to remove these trees at once to keep the disease from spreading. The slightest sign of root rot, conk or budworm presses the panic button with many foresters. I believe that he, in all sincerity, felt I was not aware of the problem. Indeed I am, and I know some of the reasons for the appearance of tree diseases. I also know that the intensive forestry practices of the industry have done much to spread infestations and disease.

In 1939 I had a budworm infestation. I was afraid it might kill my whole stand. I had just bought the land and was looking at the possibility of losing it! I had read about budworm infestations and I knew it was worse on some species, particularly spruce. That was about as much as I knew. Fortunately I was able to consult with a forester who had practised for many years.

1939 was a year of very bad infestation between Duncan and Lantzville, yet he told me not to worry! He explained that the budworm had been around the year before, more numerous than usual, and that I probably hadn't noticed. He was right. "This year is peak," he said, "Next year they will be mostly gone. Natural predators will help eradicate them, along with a dying off of their own cycle. In three years I'll pay you $50 for every budworm you find!" I was pretty surprised. I knew that this forester would not gamble half a month's salary on my budworm unless it was a sure thing. He was right again. There hasn't been any budworm since.

In the Fraser Canyon the people refused to let spraying occur during a budworm infestation. Three years later the budworm was gone. In my case, ten or twelve of the trees died and were removed in my 1945 cut. Other trees were set back due to foliage loss. They recovered and continued a healthy growth pattern.

If the government hadn't panicked when there was the budworm infestation in New Brunswick and started spraying, the problem would not have developed so severely. The spray has built up resistant worms and killed off most of the birds. Furthermore, trees could not go through their natural cycle of resistance. Plantation planting, with its "same species, same age" policy increases the susceptibility of the tree. It's like chicken-pox going through the classroom. Childhood diseases strike at certain ages, when the immune system is low to that particular stress. Trees stress too at certain ages, especially if they are nursery stock grown and planted on depleted soils.

Conk is a fungal disease which gets to the tree through the sap. The fungus forms both on the tree and on the ground. Cross pollination puts the spores into the air, rain water carries it into the ground, and it is brought up to the tree through the sap.

Conk is observed by the fruiting fungi appearing on the trunk, often called "shelf mushroom". If I see a tree with the disease, I inventory it for the next cut. However, I've known trees to last 50 years with conk. It takes a long time for the wood fiber to become spongy and in this area, it often does not devastate the whole tree. I've felled trees where the first section is fine, the second conky, and the top section is clear again. I have seldom lost the whole tree. There might be evidence of it in the butt, and the rest of the tree absolutely clear. The diseased wood can be used for marketable firewood. In 1939, active conk in Wildwood's trees was one in fifteen. By my fourth cut in 1968, conk was sited in one in thirty trees. In my ninth cut, finished in January 1990, conk was one in forty-eight trees.

Root rots are diseases caused by fungi in the root systems of trees. This micro-organism is in the soil at all times. Tree plantations of Douglas fir are very susceptible to root rot between the ages of thirty to thirty-five years. Other conifers, hemlock and balsam, are susceptible at various ages. Monocropping (single species planting) encourages the life of root rot. Once it is in a plantation, root rot is very difficult to eradicate, living in stumps for up to a century. It survives forest fires if the infected roots are insulated from the heat by the soil. The spread of this disease may be done without actual contact between the infected and healthy root systems. This organism is in the soil at all times and it is the health of the tree and the soil that determines its spread.

In 1939 root rot was apparent in one in ten trees; in 1990 it was one in twenty-five. The health of the trees are improving. Wildwood is a forest of mixed species at various ages with good spacing which makes vigorous trees. In 1945 in the area where I cut trees with root rot, the natural reseeding showed no signs of the disease. Today the trees at forty-five years of age are still healthy. I theorize clear-cut areas encourage rot because of the heating of the soil (intensive sun or fire). This may destroy controlling bacteria, leaving the fungal root rot to "flower".

The powder worm is also a pest. This worm does not like cover, and lives on the perimeter of the forest. A cedar tree away from protective cover will have a much higher probability of being infested with powder worm. For example, the cedars and balsams in the Yellowpoint area are dying out due to the recent dry years. When the soil retains plenty of moisture, these trees would gradually reseed up slopes and ridges. However, as the dry cycles occur, these trees will die out becoming hosts to the powder worm.

Vulnerability to disease is increased by the parasitic effects of dwarf mistletoe (not to be confused with the leafy mistletoe used at Christmas), particularly among western hemlock. The infection is recognizable by "witches broom", a dense tangle of branches and swelling of the trunk or branches. It spreads through a stand by ejecting at high speeds its seeds which can travel forty-five to fifty feet. The seed sticks to the tree, sending roots through the bark and into the tree to tap water and nutrients. With the exception of larch, it rarely kills the host tree, but seriously hampers the growth making it vulnerable to insects and disease. Unfortunately, the only thing I know to do is cut down the host tree and burn all residue.

I do not consider disease a problem at Wildwood. I do not worry about a one in forty ratio with conk, nor do I worry about a one in twenty with rot. There is an appearance of the disease but the trees are, in fact, getting healthier. Actually, I have one large tree showing conk which seems to be "in remission"! This was a tree where my animals bedded down. Either the nutrients put into the soil by the animals corrected the condition, or the conk receded because of a "killing" effect of the animal droppings. I don't know of any study done with this premise, but something changed the health of that tree!

My opinion is that more timber is lost in B.C. due to fire that got out of control than to disease. I've seen four to five million board feet of timber burned on Vancouver Island in one year due to these fires. The burned trees may have some purpose—they are great hosts to the insects which prefer the standing tree to one on the ground. It is very hard to get the statistics on losses due to man-set fires, yet the forestry officials are very happy to push the panic button on diseases. Maybe this is an excuse to deplete hectares of timber without looking at the natural process of control.

* * * *

January, 1995

I have stated that the only way I know to control dwarf mistletoe in hemlock is to cut the tree and burn the mistletoe. When inspecting the tree, its stunted growth and odd growth formation is obvious, but to some, this is beauty! A very enterprising architect has these trees milled on a portable mill, and the stain and grain twists of the boards bring the unusual into his expensive interiors, a graphic illustration of how we need more innovative people and smaller mills to utilize our resources. Big plantations, with no room or thought for creative thinking are letting us down.

In 1939 a forester, newly schooled in "advanced" methods of industrial forestry, told me to cut all the cedar on my property, grow fir and nothing else. The cedar I would have destroyed is now at milling age and is very valuable because of its quality grain.

I leave some western red cedar out in the open to attract the powder worm - "decoy trees". The cedars under good canopy don't become infected, or if so, very minimally. A keen-eyed sawyer (another advantage to small mills) noted how the powder worm enters the tree through dead limbs at the base of the tree. I am experimenting with removal of all dead limbs from a pilot group of cedar. It's too soon to holler BINGO! yet, but the improvement in the quality of the cedar through branch removal will pay in the long run - a win situation.

Conk is observed by the fruiting fungi appearing on the trunk…

The trees must be thinned so they will not crowd each other.

The Helping Hand

I look at Wildwood's forest as a garden running on a different time clock. It doesn't mature in a few months, but needs at least 80 years. The plants are the trees. They don't die off every year. They keep on growing. They also thrive on care and attention as do plants in a garden. Trees need the right kind of soil, light, moisture, space to grow, and protection while young. The trees in Wildwood's "garden" are a renewable resource which I harvest carefully. I make every effort to care for the forest's basic resource, the soil. The trees replace themselves quickly and efficiently.

The quality of Wildwood's trees depends also on other factors: the genetic structures of the species I wish to harvest, the suitability of the growing site, and the protection of the growing trees. Usually, with natural regeneration, nature chooses the best location. Sometimes I have to remove a small tree because the site is marginal for good growth. Evidence of stress and stagnation from competition indicate a tree needs help. Brushing, seed release, spacing, thinning, and possibly pruning (notably in the case of Christmas trees) are all necessary for the good management of Wildwood.

Frequently I am asked about brush control while the new seedlings are growing. Chemicals are out of the question. They destroy much more than the root systems of brush and are often residual, spreading to the water table. The public is right to express resistance to this type of management. It certainly has no place on Wildwood, and to my mind, no place on this planet.

Brush can compete with the growing tree, but it can also be protective and a contribution to the nutritive value of the soil. I determine the rate at which the brush grows, versus the rate at which the seedlings are growing and their ability to withstand competition. Once a tree has reached past the brush and other ground covers, it is considered "free-growing".

One method I use to control brush is the grazing of sheep. At one time I tried cattle, but they were too heavy, compacting the soil and trampling the young seedlings. They also have very large tongues which swipe up the tiny seedlings caught in the grasses as they eat. Sheep, if controlled and given supplemental feedings to stop over-grazing, are very good for brush control. I use a ratio of one animal to three acres. I watch carefully and sometimes suspend their grazing when the new foliage on the seedlings is most appetizing and susceptible to breakage.

Seedlings raised by nursery methods and planted in reforestation programs are extremely appetizing to browsing animals such as deer. Experimenting in the growth patterns of nursery raised seedlings, I have on occasion planted them. These seedlings have a different "flavor" and the deer really go for them, leaving the "wild" or naturally seeded trees alone. Perhaps there is a higher sugar content in the artificially grown seedling and the deer get addicted! Having hunted and observed deer all my life, I also know that they prefer to browse in the more open areas. Whatever the reason, massively replanted areas offer little else as food, because the land has been cleared of everything else.

Manual brushing can be done using a variety of tools by cutting or girdling the stems. Effective for weeds and brush with stems less than 3 cm. are brush hooks, machetes and Sandvik brush axes. Motorized brush cutters are used for stems less than 5 cm. and are effective with salmonberry and other brush with clumped stems. Power saws are used for larger stems.

My motto of "working with nature" is important for brush control. Once the tree is free-growing, then I leave the brush alone. As trees grow higher and the sunlight diminishes, only certain ground cover will continue. Brush species are pioneer plants whose role is to quickly occupy sites that have been cleared of vegetation.

Wildwood is a managed forest where I lend the helping hand. Like a "garden", the trees must be thinned so they will not crowd each other. On this woodlot of mixed species, and mixed ages, the practice of thinning is much less disruptive to the natural habitat of the animals and birds than it is on tree plantations. There, too much is done at once, leaving a uniform stand of trees trained for one purpose, the almighty dollar. As Wildwood's trees grow and mature, like a large extended family of different ages, the difference between my standards and those of forestry companies and officials becomes obvious. Their interference with the "process" of a forest is so horrendous that we are facing the extinction of forests as we know them. My interference is minimal and I am learning all the time.

Thinning alters a tree stand density by reducing the number of trees per acre. In order to do my job properly, I decide how many trees to remove, which ones and when. In an unmanaged forest, there will be trees that die, squeezed out by the hardier trees. Foresters consider this "lost" material since these dead trees will not be marketable. However, such dead trees are homes to insects, birds and rodents vital to the life cycle of the forest. When they fall they are essential to the replenishing of the soils. I used to be very clean, removing dead trees and fallen branches. Now I know much of this material must be left for the enrichment of the soil.

The process of the growing forest is very complex and I am learning more and more about my own management. When Chris Maser, research scientist and private consultant in sustainable forestry, conducted a workshop here, he expressed concern about depletion of my soil if not enough material is left. If this is true of a carefully managed woodlot such as Wildwood, think of what massive clear-cutting is doing throughout B.C.! I shudder at the thought. Europe's forests are suffering from depleted soils because the process of decay and return was stopped for hundreds of years. The additional lever of acid rain is bringing about a collapse of some of the third crop rotations. We must have forest areas that are never touched, as laboratories for ourselves and as holders of genetic stock for the future. We must never extinguish that heritage.

* * * *

"One has to wonder how the greatest storehouse of forest riches of all time could be so devastated in the mere 50 years we have had chain saws . . . If waste in British Columbia's forest industry were eliminated, the wood thereby saved would more than equal the trees we want to save in the few islands of beauty and harmony like the Stein, the Khutzeymateen, Carmanah, Megin and Tahsish River, and those other recently identified by (the) Wilderness Committee and Valhalla Wilderness Society as worthy of preservation . . ."

—Ruth Masters, Citizen

January, 1955

I look back at the time when *WILDWOOD, A FOREST FOR THE FUTURE* was being documented. I had some hope for change. However, the deterioration of the forests in B.C. and most of North America is leading to a disaster the like of which North America has never seen. The ice age was a natural disaster (if disaster it was) but deforestation is man-made, and it is now questionable whether nature can recover.

The warming of the water due largely to clear-cutting of millions of hectres of land at the headwaters of our rivers is killing the salmon runs. The increase of 2 degrees in the Fraser system has already taken its toll. Our authorities, in their "wisdom of ignorance" dash around looking for ridiculous answers.

At Orville Camp's sustainable forest in Oregon, I was shown an experiment he was monitoring. One acre of land had been clear-cut according to current industrial forestry methods. The day I visited, we checked thermometer readings: 103 degrees (F) in the clear-cut, 83 degrees (F) in the woods. And we wonder about global warming?

The political will to change is stubborn. Unfortunately, political will walks hand in hand with corporate will. Put the people back into the woods and remove the corporations. We can no longer afford to subsidize their huge profits from trees they did not grow and forests they cannot sustain.

The Essential Ingredient

The essential ingredient in effective woodlot management is time—a long-term perspective and a day-to-day participation in a living landscape that evolves over decades and even centuries. Good woodlot management demonstrates viable alternatives to the devastation of the current forestry practices in British Columbia where timber management has been for short term economic benefits based on the dogma of clear-cut and replant.

The North American forestry industry, for over half a century, has followed the German approach of using timber as a form of industrial agriculture. This model was fastidious in the cleaning of the forest of all debris. Fallen trees, branches and other residue were carefully removed. Spindly, suppressed looking trees were thinned out of the stand, the assumption being that these suppressed trees could not be released into a growing pattern. This left evenly-spaced, even-aged reproductively superior trees, a commercial crop which gained height and girth uniformly until it reached the top of the growth curve and became (that unholy term) "decadent". At this point, the timber was cut, like any other agricultural crop, in an intense, clearcut harvest cycle timed to match "ripening". North American industry "improved" German technology by "cleaning up" debris with slash burning which removed the problems of converting waste into useful products.

One of the first things woodlot foresters discovered was that many suppressed trees do respond to release thinning (taking out other growth to let in additional light), perhaps not as quickly as younger trees, but they responded—120 foot trees could be released to gain as much as an inch in girth annually. Conventional thinning practices, which alter the forest environment dramatically by taking out the younger trees and grooming and nurturing only those of the same age category, is based on an incorrect assumption. Many foresters using alternative methods have proven that suppressed, older trees will catch up with their dominant kin, displacing one economic argument for clear-cutting and subsequent monocropping.

Slash burning is a further brutalization of forest soil. After clear-cutting and slash burning there is no longer a forest, only the skeletal remains of degraded soil unable to support the living, breathing ecosystem of a forest.

Alternative woodlot management, as conducted at Wildwood, challenges ingrained ideas. The telescoping of forest productivity into a time frame for boardroom economics is replaced with a continual growing forest. The boardroom's cut and plant mandate is threatening not only the life of our forests, but also our social and economic well-being. Businesses judge success by "net worth". Clear-cutting reduces the net worth of a forest to zero. If that forest was old growth, it will be several hundred years at best before the original value can be obtained, several hundred years not considered on the balance sheet of the company boardroom. Alternative woodlot management understands the time-frame of a forest.

So far, management of our forests has been in the hands of those who do not recognize the forest as an ecosystem of all ages and species which are interdependent. WE TOO are dependent upon this ecosystem for clean water and air which tree plantations do not supply. Boardroom foresters cut for the product without respect for the life of the forest. The sustainable selective method is the opposite, enhancing the use of the forest and maximizing the value of the product through marketing.

Under management such as Wildwood, young trees grow side by side with the commercially valued stock. This has the advantage of matching the genetic stock of the seedlings which are naturally reseeded to the micro-site of the parent tree holding its genetic diversity.

In restocking a clearcut with new trees, drastic procedures are often used. In order to suppress weed growth (a natural part of soil regeneration) there might be an application of alumagel, derived from the Vietnam war for burning enemy territory, now used to burn clear-cuts prior to planting. After the seedlings are planted, there may be a need for further applications of herbicide to restrain competitive weeds and ground covers. There are terrific costs in such programs. These costs are being used to excuse the extraction of the maximum dollar profit from the land; the soils are devastated in the process, and ancient trees, that cost companies nothing to grow, have been essentially free for the taking. The planted "Fiber Farms", or tree plantations, have lost the genetic diversity of the old growth forests and the wisdom of nature's evolution.

The management of Wildwood contrasts strongly with the cornrow, industrial-agricultural style of tree farming. Trees for marketing are selected from a diverse natural system of hardwoods and softwoods, retaining all ages within the stand. Here is a forest profitably harvested without compromising the aesthetics of the forest environment. By maintaining such a balanced, healthy landscape, there are still abundant populations of native wildlife; eagles, pileated woodpeckers, owls, deer and a multitude of other creatures in their own habitat.

The traditional methods of forestry have been primarily interested in re-establishing trees but not the complex ecosystem of a forest. The object of woodlot management, such as Wildwood, is to retain elements of forest diversity or to reintroduce diversity. During selective logging what is left behind is of more importance than what is removed! Still standing after a cut are strong, healthy mature trees for canopy, reseeding, and as habitat for organisms ranging from microbes to vertebrates vital to the life of the ecosystem. Coarse, woody debris, large standing dead trees and downed logs provide for the diversity of organisms, all part of the chain of interdependency in the forest. A large fallen tree may take four hundred years to return to the soil, years of happy munching for bugs, organisms, birds, fungi and other life forms unknown in our books of science.

In understanding that Wildwood is an ecosystem, it is also understood that it is part of a larger ecosystem, the planet. Humans are not separate from that ecosystem. We are part of it and our lives depend on its health. It produces all life, including human.

This more sensitive, more sensible forestry, as practised at Wildwood, will be the forestry of the future, bridging areas that must now be restored to health after being brutalized, and areas of old growth that must remain untouched laboratories for restoration, heritage for all life on this planet. This bridge will involve human activity, forest productivity, and a caring for its life system. The forestry of the future holds the essential ingredients, time and patience with nature's design, a new way of thinking about one of the oldest living species on earth, the tree.

—Ruth Loomis, April 1990

February 17, 1994

Statement in the Supreme Court of British Columbia

*Merv and his wife, Anne, actively supported protests against logging the
ancient rainforest in Clayoquot Sound on the west coast of Vancouver Island.
During the summer of 1993, protesters blockaded the logging road entrance to
the rainforest, and more than 850 protesters were arrested for ignoring a B.C.
Supreme Court injunction against the blockade. On August 9, 1993, Merv and
Anne were arrested and charged with contempt of court. Their trial began in
February, 1994. Merv's statement in the Supreme Court follows.*

My Lord: I am in this Courtroom today for a number of reasons, well
considered. I am charged with criminal contempt of a Court Order. I do
not consider that any of my actions on the day of August 9th were criminal
in any regard. Therefore, I am pleading "Not Guilty".

I did not, on August 9th, do any damage to property of anyone, cause any
bodily harm to any other persons there, including the police, and did not in
any way use language offensive to anyone. By objecting in a peaceful
manner to the activities of MacMillan and Bloedel, a multinational cor-
poration with more convictions for breaking forestry laws and contravening
more regulations in their operations than all the defendants in this case put
together, I do not consider myself a criminal.

The road I was standing on has been paid for by the people of British
Columbia, either by direct grant or subsidized by ridiculously low stumpage
rates. Therefore, I was in truth standing on my own property because I, as
a citizen, have helped to subsidize MacMillan and Bloedel logging roads
for several decades. If there is indeed any measure of contempt, it is not for
the Courts as such, but for the company that devalues my country, breaks
its laws at convenience, manipulates my elected representatives, and then
uses professional truth benders (public relations) to brainwash the population (Forests Forever). What Premier in has right mind would step in and
agree to shoulder, at public expense, the costs of enforcing a very questionable corporate court ruling. There has to be manipulation present.

I believe that the record of activities over my lifetime in and on behalf of
my fellow Canadians should prove to you, my Lord, or any other worthwhile
person that I am indeed a solid citizen. I stood along with scores of like

persons on that logging road. I grew up with people and principles that told me clearly that if I saw a crime being perpetuated I should do everything in my power to stop it. Failing that, I should further work to bring the culprit to justice. I still believe this.

Now, at the age of 80 I am being told that when I see a vandal destroying my property, a thief taking my bank account, and at the same time stopping to rape the environment, that I am supposed to help by not getting in the way - why? - because he has a slip of paper allowing him to do virtually anything? My Lord, I simply do not buy into this concept of justice!

As a witness and as a spectator during this set of trials I have heard people being told they should have gone another road, should have taken other action. My Lord, I will hand you this group of documents typical of literally dozens, and in some cases hundreds, of representations to the proper people and to the press, commissions, sittings, etc., on the very issues that resulted in the Clayoquot blockade, all of which have been ignored completely or replied to in a manner that was little credit to the government, industry or any other of the forestry groups. There is a point - there always comes one - at which action becomes the only possible alternative.

We are fortunate indeed that the high calibre of the people on the Clayoquot Blockade has so far precluded the use of violence. These people faced with ridiculous slander have remained non-violent. This is more remarkable because on almost every other continent people faced with as grave an issue have chosen violence. Let's not push it.

It has been well said that the forest industry of B.C. was born in corruption, raised in corruption and seeks to maintain that corruption. We have good reason to know this. First, we took the land of the First Nations and the timber with it. In the early 1900s T.D. Pattullo gave the Powell River Company half of Graham Island tax free for 90 years. The Haida were never consulted. Robert Sommers later got 18 months for gambling away a timber license. W.C. Bennett allowed the companies to police themselves. Is it any wonder that you have more than 800 people arrested for trying to stop this type of forestry?

My Lord, it is not necessary to destroy the forest to extract timber. It is a matter of method. Many systems are available that can operate in a manner that is acceptable to the environment and environmental people. Mac-Millan and Bloedel, like all the other companies know how. I was present in a group of people some time back where a top forester for M & B told us, "The reason we won't do alternate forestry here is that we would be admitting that we know how." This statement is well known to many.

The refusal to do a proper job in the interests of foreign investors is unacceptable. Proper forestry is more a matter of using more labour and less equipment. Skullduggery by the unions and operators has blinded the average worker and the public to this fact.

In summary, there are probably as many reasons for people standing on the logging road as there were people who did so. Very bona-fide to all of them. I stood on the road because my conscience as a Canadian who loves the country I was born in compelled me to do so. Again, I could no longer stand idly by and see one of the most beautiful and productive areas of my province wiped out.

Every 322 hectares of clear-cut forest in B.C. puts one forest worker out of work for a least 150 years. Foreign foresters, basing their assessment on their own experience, refer to our methods as a complete disaster to the forest and the environment. I cannot but concur in their assessments because I, too, am a forester.

As a citizen I still am perhaps naive enough to think that there has to be some basic justice in our laws - that a dictionary of law is not necessarily the ultimate in justice. Congratulations pouring in from all over the continent and abroad tell me that I made a good decision. I am a grandfather and great-grandfather and as such I would be a traitor not to have challenged an injunction that guarantees the right to destroy.

Merv and Anne were found guilty of contempt of court, and each was sentenced to 100 hours of community service. Their probation officer would not allow them to serve their sentences in forestry work, so Merv worked with the Morrell Sanctuary in Nanaimo, and Anne worked in a retirement lodge in Cedar.

Bibliography

Carr, Emily. *Klee Wyck.* Toronto, Ont.: Irwin, 1941.

Carter, Anthony. *Abundant Rivers.* Saanichton, B.C.: Hancock House, 1972.

Franklin, Jerry, et al. *Ecological Characteristics of Old Growth Douglas Fir Forests.* Portland, Ore.: U.S. Department of Agriculture Pacific Northwest Forest and Range Experiment Station, 1981.

George, Chief Dan, and Helmut Hernschall. *My Heart Soars.* Saanichton, B.C.: Hancock House, 1974.

Gibbon, Edward. *Decline and Fall of the Roman Empire.* various.

Gould, Ed. *Logging: B.C.'s Logging Industry.* Saanichton, B.C.: Hancock House, 1975.

Kelly, David, and Gary Braasch. *The Old Growth Forest.* Salt Lake City, Utah: Peregrine Smith, 1988.

King, F.H. *Farmers of Forty Centuries.* Emmaus, Penn.: Rodale, n.d. (A reprint of a 1911 classic work on how the people of China farmed the same land for 4,000 years without destroying the soil.

Maser, Chris. *Forest Primeval.* San Francisco: Sierra Club, 1989.

Maser, Chris. *The Redesigned Forest.* San Pedro, Cal.: R. and E. Miles, 1988.

Maser, Chris, and James Trappe. *The Seen and Unseen World of the Fallen Tree.* Portland, Ore.: U.S. Department of Agriculture Pacific Northwest Range Experiment Station, 1981.

McKibben, Bill. *The End of Nature.* Toronto: Random House, 1989.

Richmond, Hector Allan. *Forever Green.* Lantzville, B.C.: Oolichan Press, 1983.

Woodcock, George. *Peoples of the Coast.* Edmonton, Alta.: Hurtig, 1977.

Young, Cameron. *Forests of British Columbia.* North Vancouver, B.C.: Whitecap, 1985.

... what is left behind is of more importance than what is removed.